WLFI*
*We've Lost Financial Independence

The **True** Genesis of
Trump's Crypto Empire
World Liberty Financial & USD1

*How the Trumps Built the First Private Central
Bank of Crypto*

LANGDON CAGE

JOY
JOY Publishing

To Truth over Perception

ISBN: 979-8-9931708-0-0 (paperback)
ISBN: 979-8-9931708-1-7 (hardcover)
ISBN: 979-8-9931708-2-4 (ebook)
LCCN: [Pending]

Published by:
JOY of Youth Publishing, LLC

Disclaimer:
This book is an independent work of journalism and commentary. It is not authorized by, affiliated with, or endorsed by World Liberty Financial, Alt5, or any other company, individual, or organization mentioned herein. All trademarks and company names are the property of their respective owners and are used solely for purposes of commentary, analysis, and reporting.

First Edition
10 9 8 7 6 5 4 3 2 1

Printed in the United States of America

Author's Note

This book is a work of narrative nonfiction with dramatized elements.

The events, entities, and financial structures described—such as World Liberty Financial (WLFI), USD1, and their connections to public figures—are drawn from publicly available information, market data, and credible reporting.

To help tell the story, certain dialogue, scenes, and characterizations have been fictionalized. One such example is 'Steve,' a composite narrator created from multiple voices, used to guide the reader through events. These narrative choices are intended to illustrate broader truths and patterns, not to assert literal transcripts or private conversations.

Nothing in this book should be read as an accusation of criminal conduct unless already established in the public record.
Where speculation or interpretation is offered, it is clearly part of the author's analysis.

The names of real people, including Donald J. Trump, members of the Trump family, and affiliated business figures, are used because they are central to matters of public concern.
This book is not authorized by, affiliated with, or endorsed by any individual or organization referenced.

The intent of this work is to document, analyze, and comment on the rise of WLFI and its surrounding ecosystem. Any fictionalized elements are employed solely to deepen the narrative and underscore the sociological, financial, and political implications of this story.

Every fact here is real. Every structure, filing, quote, and market move is verifiable.

The story you are about to read is happening in real time.

Call it a coin if you want — but it's really rails, pipes, the whole damn plumbing of money.

– Eric Trump

People don't get it yet — this isn't speculation, this is sovereignty.

– Donald Trump Jr.

World Liberty Financial isn't DeFi. It's the antidote to DeFi.

– Zach Witkoff

Prologue: What If I Told You

What if I told you the Trump family are primed to become the wealthiest people on the planet—and there's nothing you can do to stop it? This isn't hyperbole. It isn't conspiracy theory. It's not even secret. It's happening in broad daylight, plastered across CNBC headlines and TikTok feeds, printed in the Wall Street Journal and Financial Times.

It begins with a token: WLFI—World Liberty Financial. Born in the chaos of decentralized finance, branded with the Trump name, and designed to look like freedom while functioning like control. WLFI is not a cryptocurrency in the way most people imagine. It is not Bitcoin. It is not Ethereum.

Bitcoin is digital gold—a fixed supply, mined into existence through raw computing power. Its whole value rests on scarcity, on the idea that no one can make more than the algorithm allows. Ethereum is digital infrastructure—a global computer that anyone can program. It isn't about scarcity; it's about possibility. Apps, contracts, entire ecosystems are built on its rails. WLFI is neither.

It is not built on scarcity or innovation. WLFI is built on branding, liquidity loops, and political theater. It doesn't need to mine new coins or host new apps. Its foundation isn't mathematics or engineering—it's perception. The name stamped on it. The headlines wrapped around it. The illusion of inevitability.

Bitcoin created money without banks. Ethereum created apps without gatekeepers.

WLFI created nothing.

And yet, by branding itself as everything—freedom, rails, the future of finance—it positioned itself as the most powerful coin of all and minted their own money. WLFI's power doesn't come from scarcity or innovation. It comes from its twin: the stablecoin USD1

Every time its stablecoin counterpart, USD1, is minted, WLFI profits. Unlike Bitcoin, there is no cap. Unlike Ethereum, there is no open ecosystem. USD1 is elastic, printing as demand grows, each issuance feeding back into WLFI's value. Every trade on exchanges—whether it's a retail buy, a bot loop, or pure wash trading—pushes WLFI higher. Its treasury, secured through a $1.5 billion deal with the company Alt5, now holds more than half the supply. Governance votes? A mirage. "Decentralization"? A word on a website. WLFI isn't a cryptocurrency in the old sense. It's a machine, powered by branding, by volume, and by a stablecoin that guarantees it never runs dry.

And all of it is controlled by the same family that once slapped their name on casinos, steaks, and towers. Only this time, the product isn't real estate. It's money itself. WLFI isn't just another token. It is the first private central bank of crypto. And if you think that sounds terrifying, you're right.

Chapter 1: Washington in Code

I've lived around the politics of Washington, D.C. on and off my whole life. If there's one thing I know to be true: they like to talk. Washington, D.C. is a city built on language. The words carved into marble walls, whispered in hallways, slipped into bills no one reads. Language is currency here—elastic, malleable, able to reshape reality when enough people repeat it. Crypto was made for a place like this.

Try to explain it and you immediately fall into riddles. A system where every transaction is public, but ownership is hidden. A ledger everyone can see, yet no one can truly decipher. The money moves in plain sight, but the faces behind it dissolve into strings of code. Even the experts can't agree on what it is. Currency? Commodity? Security? Something else entirely?

That confusion isn't a flaw. It's the point. The more tangled the definitions, the easier it is to bend them. What can't be explained can't be regulated. And into that gray fog walked the crypto evangelists. Libertarians with manifestos about freedom. Tech bros promising disruption. Lobbyists with binders full of innovation talking points. Each group convinced they were unlocking something historic. Each group whispering the same line: this could change everything. They weren't wrong.

But where most saw code, the Trump family saw the angle. They watched industries twist themselves into knots trying to explain crypto, watched regulators stutter over definitions, watched Congress clap for words they didn't understand. To Trump, it was all familiar. He had spent a lifetime thriving on confusion— branding towers he didn't own, selling stakes in businesses he didn't control, profiting from deals where someone else carried the risk.

Crypto wasn't just another grift. It was the ultimate grift. A financial system where perception was value, where branding was collateral, where the lines between truth and illusion blurred so thoroughly that even the referees couldn't call foul.

He said it plainly once, almost like a throwaway line: We're gonna be the wealthiest country in the world. What he didn't need to say was the part everyone else missed. If Trump was the country, he was right. Because in a world this confusing, the truth doesn't belong to whoever solves the code. The truth belongs to whoever tells the story. And WLFI wasn't just telling the story—it was already writing the script.

Chapter 2: The Boys

If WLFI was a movie, you'd expect the patriarch himself to star. But Donald Trump doesn't need to be in every scene. The real operators—the ones on stage and in the clubs, at the crypto conferences and on the yachts—were the "three boys of crypto." Eric Trump. Don Jr. Zach Witkoff. They weren't Wall Street slick or Silicon Valley brilliant. They were social climbers with inherited Rolodexes, chasing the validation they'd always been denied.

Eric was the face. He'd discovered crypto like it was a second adolescence—a chance to finally be the cool kid. Ibiza yacht parties, velvet ropes in Miami, the whispered thrill of Telegram groups where "the future" was decided at 3 a.m.

Don Jr. played the hype man. Twitter rants about "owning your own rails," half-baked speeches that mashed libertarian buzzwords with MAGA talking points. He was a salesman, nothing more—but that was the point. He didn't need to understand WLFI; he just needed to make it sound inevitable.

And then there was Witkoff. The developer, the operator, the one who looked most at home on stage with a headset mic. The son of a real estate tycoon, he'd grown up on borrowed credibility and now found himself at the nexus of tech, politics, and grift. Together, they were the perfect triangle: the face, the voice, the operator.

But here's the dirty secret: none of them controlled WLFI. Not really. WLFI controlled them. The mechanics of the token, the loops of USD1, the offshore reserves—it was bigger than any one of the boys. They were just the salesmen at the front of the carnival tent, distracting you while the real machinery churned in the back.

I kept circling the same thought: WLFI looked like a coin, but it didn't feel like one. At least, not yet. There was no on-chain history to track, no wallets to map, no transactions flowing in public view. Everything I was piecing together came from whispers in Telegram chats, half-baked decks passed around at conferences, headlines that felt more like ads than reporting.

Bitcoin had scarcity baked into its code. Ethereum had an ecosystem that sprawled out like a living organism. WLFI had none of that. It had promises. Branding. Pre-market theater staged to look inevitable. Some days I thought maybe I was overthinking it. Maybe WLFI was just another coin in waiting, one more speculative bet among thousands. The kind of thing you could flip for a profit if you timed it right.

But then I'd read the fine print. Governance "votes" already dominated by insiders who hadn't released a single token. Treasury plans that talked about reserves before there was even supply. Stablecoin mechanics that seemed to mint profit out of thin air.

So what was it? A coin waiting to launch? A stock proxy in disguise? A bank stitched together out of branding and political connections? I didn't know. That was the point. The confusion wasn't a bug—it was the feature. WLFI thrived in the blur, in the space between categories where nothing fit neatly enough to regulate. And every time I tried to untangle it, the knot only pulled tighter.

Chapter 3: Gossip in Ibiza

Eric had always been the afterthought. Even among the Trump kids—hardly paragons of intellect—he carried the reputation as the "dumb one." Late-night comedians, gossip columnists, even conservative insiders all seemed to agree: Eric was second fiddle, the awkward son. If Don Jr. was the loudmouth and Ivanka the polished heir, Eric was the punchline.

What could possibly make him the cool kid? Crypto. Not because he understood it—he didn't—but because with enough money behind you, understanding wasn't required. His father had given him the one thing that mattered: permission. Permission to run with it, to stamp the Trump name on a space that thrived on confusion and complexity. You don't need to code when you can buy credibility. You don't need to innovate when you can brand. For Eric, that was the ticket. A way to step out of the shadow, not by changing who he was, but by attaching himself to the one arena where ignorance didn't disqualify you—because no one really understood it anyway.

The first time I heard Eric Trump's name tied to WLFI, it wasn't from a filing or a headline. It was gossip. Ibiza, of all places. Crypto runs on rumor, and the summer conferences had become half-tech, half-rave. Men in linen shirts and mirrored sunglasses spilled out of yachts into velvet-roped parties, still buzzing from the bass of the clubs. Deals were whispered over champagne flutes. Telegram group admins—barely out of college—suddenly found themselves treated like market makers. And somewhere in the mix was Eric.

"Eric's really leaning in," one guy said, tipping his glass in a private villa rented for the week. "Ibiza's his second adolescence. Crypto's giving him what politics never did—he gets to be the cool kid." The others laughed, nodded. Nobody questioned it. Ibiza was different—looser, more reckless, a place where image meant everything. Eric was chasing that image hard.

I watched a clip later, shaky phone footage uploaded from a conference panel. Eric onstage, shirt just a little too tight, sweat beading under the lights. He leaned into the microphone, his voice trembling, not from nerves but from the thrill of finally being taken seriously. "Decentralization is freedom," he said. "WLFI is freedom." The room broke into applause. Not the kind of applause that comes from conviction, but the kind that comes from calculation. They weren't clapping because they believed it. They were clapping because they knew the afterparty would be stocked with billionaires, champagne, and access.

That was the pattern with Eric. The words were hollow. The room knew it. He probably knew it. But none of that mattered. The performance was the point. Every time he stepped on a stage, or leaned into a mic, it wasn't about the content—it was about the echo. But to be taken seriously—even if only for the length of a headline or a shaky Instagram story—was everything. Crypto was his shot. Not because he understood it—he didn't—but because the room believed he did. And that was enough.

WLFI was the ticket that got him through the door. Not a token yet, not a system yet, but an idea. An invitation to a world where the right branding and the right access could turn even hollow words into power.

Chapter 4: One-on-One

The thing about gossip is that it makes great theater. But gossip doesn't explain mechanics. And mechanics were what I needed. One afternoon, I found myself on a basketball court with Marcus, a friend who worked in finance. We were running one-on-one, late afternoon, the blacktop still warm from the sun. The ball echoed sharp against the pavement.

"You're missing it," Marcus said, catching his breath, sweat streaking his forehead. "WLFI doesn't need to be valuable. It just needs to look valuable. That's the loop."

I dribbled, confused. "Loop?"

Marcus smiled, stole the ball, drove to the hoop. Easy layup. "Closed circuit. They mint USD1, they use USD1 to buy WLFI, WLFI props up USD1. Round and round. Value created from movement, not substance." I leaned against the fence, panting. "So they just… keep cycling it? Like an illusion?"

"Exactly," Marcus said, wiping his palms on his shorts. "It's like playing HORSE with yourself—you always win. And as long as the scoreboard keeps ticking, everyone else thinks you're in a real game." The metaphor hit harder than the ball. It bounced once, twice, rolling into the dark corner of the court. Neither of us chased it. Then it hit me. The way the whole thing resembled the game we weren't even playing anymore. Marcus and I could pretend the shots mattered, that we were in control of the score. But the truth was, the hoop didn't care. The court didn't care. And if someone else owned the ball? We were just running in circles.

That's when I realized the gossip about Eric wasn't just fluff. Ibiza was theater, but the mechanics were the trick. The "cool kid" act was a distraction while the machine whirred in the background. Crypto loves to sell you freedom. But behind the curtain, it was just a handful of players passing the ball to themselves, racking up fake points, and laughing while the crowd cheered.

Chapter 5: Don Jr. Speaks

If Eric was chasing the thrill of finally being taken seriously, Don Jr. was chasing something darker—the sound of power.

The Miami ballroom wasn't glamorous. The lights were too bright, the air stale from the buffet. Rows of suits and dresses shuffled in, half-buzzed on cocktails, half-hungover from the night before. They weren't there for substance. They were there to gauge the room. To watch. To whisper. When Don Jr. walked out, there wasn't a rush of applause. There was a ripple of skepticism. The kind you can feel when a crowd is already smirking before you open your mouth.

He launched into the script: decentralized freedom, new rails, power to the people. But the words fell flat. A man in the front row leaned back in his chair, smirking at his colleague. A woman two rows back checked her phone. You could feel the contempt—polite, but unmistakable. Don Jr. felt it too. His jaw clenched. His delivery sharpened, louder, more insistent. Then came the break.

"Banks rejected us!" he snapped, anger bleeding through the polish. "We were erased. Took our insurance away. So we built something that can't be controlled." The room shifted. The whispers quieted. Heads turned.

He pressed on, voice lower now, but colder. "This is ours. They can't shut us out if we own the rails." It wasn't rhetoric anymore. It was confession. Revenge dressed up as innovation.

And then, the line that sealed it: "I've watched headlines spin. They don't know how this works. But they see the logos, they see charts flashing, and they believe." Silence. A beat too long. Everyone in the room understood what he'd just said.

This wasn't about decentralization. It wasn't about freedom. It was about manipulation—weaponizing perception, branding, volume, and headlines to build an empire.

And then the applause came. Hesitant at first, then swelling. Not because anyone disagreed. Not because they were inspired. They clapped because they recognized the truth and accepted it. That was the part that lodged in my chest like a stone: They were confessing. And no one cared.

Chapter 7: After Miami

The bar was filled with graduate students and young Capitol Hill staffers all debating, complaining, or outright bitching. One of those happy hour spots that everyone goes to, but no one really likes. It's just, the place. The corner by the dart boards was the least crowded spot. Marcus lined up for his throw, all calm shoulders and focus. Lizzy, on the other hand, was a live wire—dart in one hand, pint in the other, pacing like she was about to debate Congress.

"Okay, you've got to explain this to me again," she said, glaring at the dartboard like it owed her money. "Crypto. Because I swear, if one more guy in my office corner-slacks me with, 'Have you looked at Solana?' I'm going to set the break room Keurig on fire." Marcus snorted. "Rough day?"

"Rough? ROUGH? Try surviving six hours of listening to Brad from accounting call himself a 'DeFi crusader' while I'm literally trying to get payroll done. He bought Bitcoin once in 2017 and suddenly he's a freedom fighter." She took a long sip, wiped her mouth with the back of her hand, and let it rip. "Bitcoin, Ethereum, Doge, Shiba—what the hell is this alphabet soup? I mean, come on. Pirate money, nerd money, joke money, puppy money. And somehow my little brother—MY LITTLE BROTHER—made a million dollars on Dogecoin. The guy can't even fold laundry. He still thinks Hot Pockets are a food group!" Her dart missed the board entirely, clattering against the jukebox. Marcus laughed. "That's about as accurate as Dogecoin."

Lizzy spun back toward us, finger stabbing the air like she was cross-examining the universe. "No, listen. I've got this. Bitcoin was pirate money. Ethereum was nerd money. And WLFI…" She paused dramatically, eyes going wide, lips curling into a grin like she was about to crack the Da Vinci Code. "…WLFI is the bank. Oh my God. It's the BANK." Marcus and I froze.

She barreled on, faster, louder, energized now like she'd mainlined Red Bull. "Think about it! Not a coin, not a product—a casino chip. You hand them your money, they hand you a shiny token, and suddenly you're in their system. Every trade, every swap, every loser who thinks they're the lucky one—they're the fuel! That's the whole grift! That's—" She gasped theatrically, clutching her chest. "Wait. Wait. What if it's worse? What if the whole thing's run by, like, DARPA cyborgs who plant chips in your Visa card? What if Trump's hair is actually the antenna?!" Marcus nearly dropped his beer. "Jesus, Lizzy."

Lizzy's energy getting louder, "No! Hear me out! They'll make us use USD1 for everything. Groceries, gas, Amazon. And every time we swipe, BOOM—they clone our DNA. And who buys it? Elon Musk! To make crypto babies on Mars! Tiny crypto astronauts with little WLFI logos for pupils!" Her voice cracked on the last word, dart grasped in her hand by the tail, pointed like she might stab the air itself. The bar went dead silent. Marcus coughed into his pint. I just blinked at her. Deadpan, "You good?"

She dropped into her chair, panting like she'd run a marathon, then grinned. "So… am I close?" Lizzy burst out laughing, the kind that made heads turn. Marcus shook his head, chuckling, muttering something about "crypto babies." But me? I wasn't laughing.

Because buried in all her madness—wedged between pirate money, nerd money, and crypto babies on Mars—Lizzy had stumbled onto something that no CNBC anchor, no Bloomberg columnist, no Telegram "alpha leaker" had managed to say out loud.

WLFI is the bank. Not a coin. Not an app. Not some plucky little startup riding the wave of "innovation." A bank.

The words rattled around in my head like loose change. The part that hit hardest wasn't that she'd said it—it was that she'd said it without even knowing what it meant. She was half-drunk, ranting about Hot Pockets and conspiracies, and still managed to cut through the noise with more clarity than entire think tanks in Washington.

That's what WLFI was becoming. A private central bank hiding in plain sight. Built on branding instead of reserves, memes instead of monetary policy, Telegram threads instead of Treasury bills. Every USD1 token minted was another brick in the vault. Every trade on Binance or Gate, real or bot, was another toll on the highway. Lizzy didn't know it. Hell, maybe nobody knew it—not really. But the mechanics were all pointing in the same direction.

It was the Al Capone problem. The man had owned half of Chicago, bribed cops, run booze across state lines, and no one could touch him. But in the end, it wasn't the smuggling or the murders that got him. It was the ledgers. The paperwork. The boring math that nobody looked at until it was too late.

That's what WLFI felt like. A carnival on the outside—foam parties, yachts, Instagram clips of Eric yelling "Crypto never sleeps!"—but in the back room, the ledgers told the real story. And the story was simple: this wasn't decentralization. This was consolidation. A few names holding the pen, deciding how much ink to spill.

Lizzy went back to throwing darts, laughing at her own Mars theory. Marcus rolled his eyes and chalked his cue for a game of pool. The bar noise swelled again—jukebox, clinking glasses, someone shouting for another round. But me? I stayed stuck on those four words, like a song I couldn't turn off.

WLFI is the bank.

Said once, like a joke. Heard once, like a punchline. But underneath, it was the only truth that mattered.

16

Chapter 8: Washington Theater

Washington is nothing if not theater. One stage, three acts.

Act One: GENIUS.

Act Two: CLARITY.

Act Three: Anti-CBDC.

Three bills, three standing ovations, three nails in the coffin of the old system.

Act One: GENIUS. Government Endorsed National Infrastructure for Unified Stablecoins. GENIUS. Einstein would be turning over in his grave.

It was pitched as protection—protection from China, protection from Wall Street, protection from the "deep state." The word freedom was practically wallpapered across every slide and press release—a drinking game waiting to happen. If you took a shot every time someone in Congress said "freedom," you'd pass out before the House vote.

The hypocrisy was on full display. To crypto insiders, "freedom" meant finally cracking open the regulatory cage and letting digital dollars flow—ideally back into their own wallets. To policymakers who barely knew a blockchain from a bicycle chain, it was a safe buzzword, a slogan they could repeat without understanding the tech.

Take Senator Elizabeth Warren. She didn't just offer mild criticism—she tore into the bill's glaring loopholes and flat-out warned it would let insiders become their own regulators, "the regulator of his own financial company and, importantly, the regulator of his competitors."

It's a perfect tension: lawmakers passing "freedom"-branded legislation they don't comprehend, while the bill's true beneficiaries—crypto firms, disruptors, self-dealers—stand to gain. And yet, thanks to the word's flexibility, no one looked bad supporting it. The result? GENIUS passed with startling speed, wrapped in calls for innovation and dollar dominance—a moment of political theater masquerading as policy.

I sat hunched over my laptop, watching C-SPAN flicker in the sickly glow of 2 a.m. The fatigue was real, and then I switched over to Fox News. There was Rep. Warren Davidson, suit crisp, confidence laser-steady, pontificating that "cryptocurrency is 'freedom money'"—as if "freedom money" were a taxable category on your 1040. That line—freedom money—landed like a pie in the face. The studio nodded along like they'd just heard the mayor's State of the Union. Meanwhile, I was mentally screaming: "He doesn't even know what he's talking about!"

But that was the beauty—and the horror—of the whole operation. Comprehension wasn't the goal. Performance was. The show mattered more than the substance. You didn't have to understand a ledger or a node or a stablecoin peg. You just had to look confident, side-eye the "deep state," and repeat buzzwords like "freedom" until people believed you had the map.

WLFI's lobbyists had written the script for them. The bill's real function wasn't to protect—it was to anoint. With GENIUS passed, USD1 wasn't just a chip in the casino anymore. It was a chip stamped Made in America. It carried the legitimacy of Congress, even though Congress had no clue what it had just handed over. I scribbled in my notebook:

GENIUS = federal blessing for WLFI's printing press.

The vote passed. The chamber applauded, staffers grinned, cameras flashed.

From the outside, it looked like triumph—patriotism wrapped in procedure. But the truth was simpler, and uglier. The people voting didn't understand what they'd just blessed. They didn't need to. WLFI's lobbyists had done the work for them, handing over the script line by line. GENIUS wasn't genius. It was the con, dressed up in red, white, and blue.

Chapter 9: CLARITY

Washington moved on from GENIUS like it was just another day at the office. Headlines flared for a second, then faded. But behind the curtain, Act Two was already on deck: CLARITY: Crypto Legal Asset Reform for Institutional Transparency and Yield. They love their acronyms. And the irony was thick here too—because if GENIUS gave WLFI a stamp of approval, CLARITY gave them cover.

I was at brunch when I tried explaining it. A classy staple of M street in Georgetown that welcomed elites and college students alike. Sunlight peaked through the logo-stained windows, coffee cups clinking. My old college friend Sara, a policy think tank devotee, sat across from me next to her boyfriend—Eli—some mid-level staffer who always wore the look of a guy afraid to say the wrong thing. The relationship made as much sense as the topic. I tore into my pancakes like I hadn't eaten in days, words spilling out.

"Surely these geniuses would have some clarity about the damage they just did, right? I mean, this bill—CLARITY—it basically says WLFI isn't a stock, isn't a currency, isn't a commodity. It's… nothing. Which means it's everything. They slipped out of every single regulatory net."

Sara arched an eyebrow, smirking. "That sounds like half the companies in this town."

Eli shook his head. "Actually, it's worse," he said quietly, like he was afraid the other tables might hear. "I've seen the language. The whole thing was ghostwritten. Not by Treasury. Not by the SEC. By lobbyists." Annoyed, I dropped my fork. "WLFI lobbyists?" He didn't answer, but his silence was enough. The waitress refilled our mugs, and for a moment the world was just clatter and the smell of bacon. Then Eli leaned in.

"You have to understand—members of Congress don't get crypto. They don't want to. Half of them can't tell a blockchain from a blender. So when someone shows up with a ready-made bill, patriotic branding, bullet points about innovation and jobs—

boom. They run with it." Sara sipped her coffee, smirking again. "You're saying it's theater."

"It's always theater," Eli said. "And WLFI just bought them the Broadway real estate." I pushed my plate away, appetite gone.

GENIUS had been the blessing. CLARITY was the disappearing act. WLFI wasn't just bigger than the Fed now. They were beyond the law.

Chapter 10: The Weight of Two Acts

I couldn't shake it. GENIUS had stamped WLFI's casino chips with the stars and stripes. CLARITY had lifted them out of regulation's reach. Two acts of theater, passed without so much as a serious debate.

I sat alone in my apartment, blinds half-drawn, the glow of my laptop painting the walls. The news was a blur of other crises—Ukraine, gas prices, some senator's scandal-of-the-week. No one was talking about WLFI. How had it gotten this far? Was it really possible Congress had just signed off on the creation of a private central bank—without even realizing it? Was I overreacting?

I pulled up a chart of stablecoins. USD1 wasn't the only player in the game. Tether, USDC—giants already holding billions. And governments weren't asleep. China already had its digital yuan, state-backed and fully operational. Surely the U.S. would roll out its own Central Bank Digital Coin (CBDC), right? Surely, WLFI would just get lost in the shuffle. We'll be fine, I told myself, running a hand over my face. There's no way a private token can outrun entire governments. Not when the Fed has the ultimate hammer. I leaned back, trying to let that thought calm me. The noise of the city drifted in through the window: a car horn, a siren in the distance, the hum of life moving on.

Then my phone buzzed. A headline. HOUSE PASSES ANTI-CBDC BILL IN LANDSLIDE VOTE. My stomach dropped. Shit. That was Act Three. The trapdoor. The final piece. Because if GENIUS gave WLFI legitimacy, and CLARITY gave them immunity, then Anti-CBDC did something far worse. It kneecapped the competition.

The government wasn't going to make its own digital dollar anymore. The Fed's shot at building a rival stablecoin was dead. Which meant USD1—WLFI's Trojan Horse—wasn't going to get lost in the shuffle. It was the shuffle. I stared at the headline, the weight of it pressing down like a brick on my chest. We weren't fine. We were screwed.

Chapter 11: Act Three — Anti-CBDC

The bar smelled like stale beer and fryer grease, the kind of place where politics was just background noise on a muted TV. Marcus nursed a whiskey, scrolling his phone, while I hunched over a pint of IPA I wasn't drinking. I couldn't keep it in anymore.

"They killed it," I said.

Marcus looked up. "Killed what?"

"The Fed's digital dollar. The CBDC. The one thing that could've kept WLFI in check. It's dead. Congress passed the Anti-CBDC bill tonight. Landslide."

He shrugged, unimpressed. "So? Who cares? Nobody wants the government spying on their bank account."

"That's the sell," I snapped, slamming my glass down harder than I meant to. "That's the pitch they used. Freedom. Privacy. No Big Brother digital dollar. But here's the truth: killing the Fed's stablecoin doesn't protect you. It hands the entire market to private players. To WLFI."

Marcus frowned, finally setting his phone down. "You're saying…?"

"I'm saying the U.S. just kneecapped itself. China has a government-backed coin. Europe's working on one. Every major economy is building rails. And we just took ours out back and shot it."

I leaned in, voice low, urgent. "GENIUS gave WLFI legitimacy. CLARITY gave them immunity. And now Anti-CBDC killed their only rival. It's game over, Marcus. The government just handed the keys to Trump's private central bank and said, 'Go nuts.'"

He stared at me like I'd lost it. "Come on. You really think Congress would just—"

"They already did," I cut him off. "And you heard Don Jr.: "It's the future of American hegemony…our economic might." He wasn't bluffing. He was telling the truth. And now? Nothing's in their way."

The bartender dropped the check between us. Marcus, unusually, didn't reach for it. For the first time since I'd started this whole dive, he didn't look skeptical. He looked scared. I drained my glass, the bitter taste catching in my throat. The third act was over. The curtain had fallen. And WLFI was the only one left standing on the stage.

Chapter 12: The Victory Party

News broke on a Wednesday. By Friday, Eric was on a jet to Palm Beach.

There were no press releases, no victory speeches on the Hill. That wasn't how WLFI operated. Their stage wasn't Congress—it was the afterparty.

The Mar-a-Lago ballroom pulsed with bass, chandeliers rattling as if they were hanging over Ibiza instead of Florida. Clips trickled onto Instagram: Eric in a velvet jacket, holding court with crypto bros and hedge funders, glass in hand. Don Jr. at the mic, grinning wide enough to split his face, railing against "Big Brother's coin" the way he always did, the crowd cheering him on. It wasn't official language, but the message was clear: the Anti-CBDC vote was theirs. A win.

Eric soaked it in. On social, he wasn't the awkward Trump kid anymore—he was the king of the room. Champagne bottles uncorked, women shrieking and posing for selfies with him, one shouting "W-L-F-I!" The chant caught like wildfire, echoing off the marble walls in shaky, blown-out phone audio.

In a corner, Zach Witkoff wasn't dancing. He was bent over a cocktail table, gesturing animatedly, scribbling numbers on a napkin for a Miami real estate guy. From the snippets I could lip-read later, it was all about the Anti-CBDC bill: how killing the Fed's option meant no competition. "Every stablecoin flows back to us. It's like owning the only casino in Vegas." The real estate guy nodded, wide-eyed, like he'd just been handed a cheat code for the future. That was the mood of the night: inevitability. They weren't just celebrating a bill. They were celebrating the illusion of untouchability.

Scrolling Instagram later, I watched the clips on repeat. The video quality was shaky, the sound distorted, but the images told the story. The villains weren't hiding. They didn't have to. And in that ballroom, for the first time, they looked like they believed it too.

Chapter 13: The Unlock Game

The victory parties were loud. The real game was quiet. WLFI's governance board wasn't glamorous. No neon lights, no DJs. Just a gray forum with usernames like CryptoPatriot1776 and HODLerForLife. Supposedly, this was the beating heart of "community-driven governance." To me, it felt like the world's most boring casino pit. Most days, the place was flooded with memes—rocket emojis, grainy gifs of Trump riding a bull, endless chatter about "wen moon." But that night, buried between the noise, a thread lit up: Unlock Proposal Discussion.

I scrolled, heart pounding. This wasn't a meme war. This was the backroom. Users debated when insiders should release their locked tokens. The numbers were already moving on-chain—you could watch them dance across Etherscan, the end-all-be-all of blockchain tracking—but here, on the board, it was like catching whispers behind the curtain.

I typed under a throwaway handle: *Isn't it a conflict if insiders are controlling the schedule?* Almost instantly, a reply:

ConcernedSupporter88:
Not at all. They're just protecting the market. If they dumped everything at once, WLFI would crash. The unlocks keep it healthy.

I leaned forward, tapping harder. *But who decides the timing? It looks like the same wallets always move first.*

ConcernedSupporter88:
Those are trusted early partners. Long-term holders. They want WLFI to succeed. We should be grateful they're not unloading the whole bag.

My chest tightened. *So they can sell whenever they want? At prices we don't even know?*

ConcernedSupporter88:
Think of it like training wheels. They're guiding the market until we're strong enough to ride alone.

I sat back, staring at the screen. Training wheels. That was the spin. But the chain of transactions on my other monitor told a different story. Wallets linked to insiders were already timing their exits with each cycle—lining up unlocks with flashy announcements, fake partnerships, rumors dropped just long enough to pump the price. Retail bought in on hype, and insiders fed on the exit. It wasn't guidance. It was harvesting.

I typed one last line: *What happens when the training wheels never come off?*

No reply. The thread rolled on, swallowed by rocket emojis and GIFs of Trump in a cape. But I already knew the answer. The wheels weren't training wheels. They were shackles. And we were the ones locked in.

Chapter 14: Offshore

If Mar-a-Lago was for show, the Caymans were for business. The photos never made the news. They weren't supposed to. A grainy shot leaked through a bored waitress—Eric and Don Jr. at a long teak table on the terrace of a resort that cost more per night than most people's mortgages. The ocean behind them was perfect, turquoise, still. The kind of water you only see in bank commercials. And that was fitting, because this was banking. The new kind.

Zach Witkoff sat at the head of the table, sunglasses perched like he'd been born with them. His napkin was covered in scrawled numbers, arrows connecting boxes, the faint outline of something big. He was explaining liquidity funnels the way most people explain a dessert menu.

"The offshore pool is essential," he said, stabbing at the napkin. "You can't just keep USD1 reserves sitting in New York. Too many eyes. Too many hands. But here? We can wrap BTC, ETH, even competitor stables, loop them back into USD1 issuance. Nobody sees the flow. Nobody asks questions."

Don Jr. leaned in, grinning, hair slicked back from the salt air. "So the more they trade, the more we make. Even when they lose, we make. Right?"

"Exactly." Witkoff smiled thin. "Closed circuit. But bigger. Offshore means leverage. The kind you can't do under SEC windows."

Eric raised his glass, eyes glittering. "Gentlemen, we're not building a coin. We're building the rails. And the world's going to pay tolls to ride." They clinked glasses, laughter rolling across the terrace. A waiter brought fresh bottles, smiling politely as if he hadn't just overheard the blueprint for a private central bank.

I studied the photo later, late at night, zooming in until the pixels blurred. The napkin with Witkoff's scribbles. Don Jr.'s manic grin. Eric's raised glass. It looked like a vacation snapshot. But to me, it was evidence. The boys of crypto weren't just celebrating anymore. They were conspiring. And they'd chosen the perfect place to do it—far from Washington, far from oversight, in a paradise where money and secrecy flowed as freely as the rum.

The offshore deal wasn't rumor. It was reality. And it made everything back home—the speeches, the bills, the hashtags—look like exactly what they were. Theater.

Chapter 15: The Bot Wars

Back home, my evidence wasn't crystal waters and champagne. It was charts.

The numbers didn't add up. Every chart, every price feed, every supposed "market cap" of WLFI—it was all smoke and mirrors. Volume spiked out of nowhere, then vanished. Wallets traded back and forth like actors reading from a script. One minute the order books looked alive; the next, they were a graveyard.

I stared at the screen until my eyes ached. It felt like I was watching shadows dance on a cave wall, trying to convince myself it was reality. That's when the memory hit.

I was twelve, hunched over the family desktop, playing an online shooter that ate up entire weekends. The servers were wild, chaotic—until the bots showed up. They didn't play like people. They moved too fast, aimed too perfectly, spawned in places that broke the rules. I'd empty a clip, thinking I'd won, only to realize I'd been shooting at code.

WLFI felt the same.

I typed on the governance board, same throwaway handle as before: *Why does volume look fake? Who's trading with who? A reply popped up, almost too fast.*

ConcernedSupporter88:
It's liquidity provisioning. Standard practice. Bots keep the market healthy.

I laughed out loud. Healthy. These weren't "market makers." They were the same bots from my childhood, coded to win before the game even loaded. Retail traders thought they were playing against each other, like kids running around in that old shooter. But the truth? The house had stacked the server. I scrolled transaction logs: $500 swaps sliced into twenty micro-trades. A $2,000 order front-run by a bot in less than a second, leaving the human buyer with crumbs at a higher price. Smoke and mirrors dressed up as "liquidity."

On the message board, I pushed again: *But if the bots are winning, how does anyone else profit?* Silence. Then, finally:

ConcernedSupporter88:
That's not the point. The point is volume. Visibility. People think WLFI is liquid, and that's what matters. Perception is reality.

I leaned back, staring at the glow of my screen.
Perception is reality.

That wasn't just a line on a message board. It was the whole blueprint.

The trades, the charts, the bots—they weren't the product. They were the billboard. The illusion of activity, the smoke and mirrors that made WLFI look like the busiest casino on earth. Then, realization. Trump had never been in the business of building things. Not really. He was in the business of branding them. Slap the name on the tower, the steaks, the university, the airline. Half of it didn't even exist. What mattered was that people believed it did. WLFI was the golden ticket. A brand masquerading as a bank, a perception masquerading as money. The Trump family had found the ultimate licensing deal: a financial system where the logo itself was the value. They didn't need to own the skyscraper. They just needed you to believe they did.

And for the first time, I understood: WLFI wasn't playing the game of crypto. WLFI was the game. The rest of us were just buying tickets to watch.

Chapter 16: The Brand

The ballroom smelled like cigars and expensive perfume, the kind of scent you couldn't wash off even if you wanted to. Miami had become the unofficial capital of crypto hype—clubs by night, conferences by day, and in between, invite-only "fireside chats" where the real business happened. This wasn't on C-SPAN. There were no official transcripts. Just a few hundred whales, influencers, and VC sharks sipping overpriced cocktails under soft orange lights. But in Miami, nothing stayed private for long. Clips hit Instagram Stories before the night was even over. TikToks spliced in emojis. Snippets leaked onto X, grainy audio under captions like "Trump boys lay out the plan."

Eric spoke first. His voice was eager, carrying that quiver of someone who'd finally found a stage where people actually cheered for him. "Look, my dad built buildings. Hotels, casinos, towers—you name it. But here's the truth: the real money wasn't in concrete. It was in the name. The brand. You slap TRUMP on it, and suddenly it's worth ten times more." Laughter rippled through the room. Glasses clinked. You could almost hear the nods, the scribbles in leather-bound notebooks. Don Jr. jumped in before the applause died. He thrived on this, playing the hype man, grinning wide as he spun the con.

"WLFI is the same play. It's not about code, or tech, or some nerdy blockchain shit. It's about the brand. People don't care if it's decentralized. Half of them don't even know what that means. What they care about is perception. And perception is reality." The audience leaned in. Some smiled knowingly, others just glazed with greed.

Eric raised his glass, doubling down. "It's our golden ticket. We don't need to own the skyscraper—we just need everyone to believe we do. And now? The whole financial system is the skyscraper." That line cracked like thunder. A roar of applause followed, echoing off the chandeliers. Someone shouted, "TO THE MOON!" Another voice added, "TRUMP MONEY, BABY!" The room fed off itself. Whales in tailored suits clapped like frat boys. Influencers filmed themselves nodding sagely, ready to chop the moment into thirty-second socials. A couple of VCs I recognized—faces from Twitter threads and podcast circuits—

whispered excitedly, already calculating how to spin this into a Series A pitch for whatever side project WLFI blessed.

In the back, a DJ who'd played Coachella once was cueing up a beat. Because why not? In Miami, business was always half-party, half-cult. And in the middle of it all, Eric and Don Jr. beamed. They weren't just selling a token. They were selling belief.

Later that night, I scrolled through the clips, the shaky phone videos and captioned tweets. Each replay hit harder. This was the playbook. WLFI wasn't a financial system—it was a brand. And the Trump family had figured out the greatest licensing deal in history: money itself. The crowd's cheers still echoed in my head when I closed my laptop. They believed. And that was all WLFI needed.

Chapter 17: Brand as Value

The clips rattled me. Not because they were surprising—if anything, they confirmed what I already suspected—but because of how quickly the words turned into reality. Exchanges lit up within days. Binance, Gate, Bitget—suddenly WLFI banners plastered across their homepages like it was the only token that mattered. Marketing deals rolled out, most of them paper-thin. Partnerships with influencers; TikTokers dancing under "#WLFI" captions. Even CNBC chimed in. A smiling anchor asked if WLFI was "the future of American crypto," parroting talking points lifted straight from the boys' Miami stage show. And behind it all? Nothing had changed. No new product. No new tech. Just the brand.

I scrolled Twitter—sorry, X—watching hashtags trend. #WLFI, #OwnTheRails, #TrumpMoney. Bots juiced the numbers, but humans piled on too. Half believed it was their ticket to riches. The other half mocked it as a scam. WLFI didn't care. Either way, the brand was winning. And the partnerships? Smoke and mirrors. One "exchange integration" turned out to be nothing more than a banner ad. A "governance alliance" was just a photo op. But perception was reality. The markets spiked anyway. I jotted in my notebook:

WLFI = Value = Brand = Perception.

I closed my eyes and heard Eric's voice again, echoing from Miami: The whole financial system is the skyscraper. And for the first time, I wondered if they were right.
I couldn't stop scrolling. Everywhere I looked, WLFI was there. Exchange banners influencers, podcasts suddenly dropping "World Liberty Financial" between ad reads for CBD gummies and sports betting apps. It was like the oxygen had been replaced. You couldn't breathe without inhaling WLFI.

But when I dug in—when I actually followed the money— the substance wasn't there. That "partnership" with a European exchange? A glorified banner ad package, rebranded as an "integration." The influencer campaign? Half the videos came from bots—AI-generated faces shilling "Trump's crypto" to audiences that didn't even exist. The supposed "advisory council"?

Just a photo-op with three minor politicians who probably thought they were shaking hands at a Chamber of Commerce breakfast.

None of it was real. And yet… it was working. Every headline, every meme, every fake collab—it pushed the narrative forward. WLFI wasn't winning on tech, or liquidity, or even governance. It was winning on branding. I scribbled in my notebook, underlined three times:

Trump Tower ≠ concrete. Trump Tower = logo.
WLFI ≠ finance. WLFI = logo.

That was the scam. That was the genius. They'd taken the oldest Trump trick—slapping the name on something hollow and selling the illusion—and scaled it to money itself.

I pulled up an Etherscan chart again. Volume spikes, but no clear buyers. Wallets trading with themselves, bots juicing numbers. The same money circling the drain, but on paper it looked like momentum. And CNBC? They ran a segment that morning calling WLFI "the fastest-growing financial product in America." Not one anchor mentioned that most of the growth was just smoke bouncing off mirrors. The brand had become the value.

I leaned back, sick to my stomach. It wasn't about whether WLFI was valuable. It was about whether people believed it was. And people did. Because the name was enough. The illusion wasn't just for retail anymore. The exchanges weren't dupes. They were in on it. Listing WLFI wasn't charity—it was a payday. Every token that wanted a banner on Binance or Kraken had to fork over listing fees that ran into the millions. WLFI wasn't being "welcomed" into the fold; it was buying its way in. And the exchanges needed it. The hype meant volume, and volume meant fees. WLFI was a cash register they couldn't afford not to ring.

The influencers weren't dupes either. They didn't need to understand liquidity pools or governance tokens. All they needed was a check and a script. I saw it play out in real time: identical tweets, same hashtags, same talking points—copy-pasted by people who'd sell detox tea one day and "Trump's crypto" the next. They didn't care if it was hollow. They cared about clicks.

It wasn't just the exchanges or the influencers. The part that twisted my stomach was the media. CNBC didn't run WLFI stories because they believed in the tech—they ran them because Trump + crypto = ratings. Bloomberg dropped op-eds that sounded like they were ghostwritten by WLFI's PR team. Even the Wall Street Journal, the place I thought would be immune, framed USD1 as a patriotic bulwark against China.

When I traced the coverage back, the fingerprints were everywhere. A CNBC "segment" turned out to be sponsored content buried in their business package deals. A Bloomberg "analysis" recycled lines word-for-word from a WLFI press release. Even Forbes ran a glowing profile of Eric Trump as "crypto's unlikely champion." I checked the author—he'd done branded content before. It was advertising dressed up as reporting.

The more I saw it, the more I realized how invisible it was to the average reader.

To them, WLFI was being covered the same way Apple or Tesla was covered. Not as a scam, not as a brand campaign, but as reality. I wrote in my notebook:

Step 1: Buy the headline.
Step 2: Let belief do the rest.

The illusion wasn't just alive—it was legitimized. Not because it was true, but because it was printed in black ink on white paper and said out loud by people in ties under studio lights. Trump had always been a master of branding. But with WLFI, he'd found the cheat code. The brand wasn't just valuable—it was newsworthy. And in America, if it's on the news, it might as well be real.

Chapter 18: Headlines

Palm Beach was heavy with humidity that night, but inside Mar-a-Lago's dining room the air was chilled to perfection. Mahogany tables gleamed under chandeliers, white-jacketed servers floated by with trays of champagne, and the soft hum of conversation carried the tone of a victory lap. Don Jr. was the loudest at the table, as always. He slapped a copy of the Wall Street Journal down with a flourish, the paper still damp from his drink. A red Sharpie had circled a headline like a coach diagramming a play: "WLFI: The People's Alternative to Central Banking."

"You see this?" he crowed, voice pitched just high enough to draw attention from nearby tables. "Front page. Legacy media. Not Breitbart, not some Telegram echo chamber. The Journal." He tapped the headline like it was proof of divinity. "We're legitimate now." The men around him laughed, raising glasses. A couple of hedge-fund types leaned in, grinning like schoolboys at the cool kid's table. Eric reclined in his chair, posture loose, smug grin curling. "And the best part? We didn't even have to pay for that one."

Witkoff, precise even in his gloating, swirled his bourbon lazily. "Not directly, anyway," he said, lips curling into a half-smile. "Let's just say when half your ad budget flows through Bloomberg, they remember how to treat you." The line landed like a private joke, triggering another round of laughter.

Eric pulled out his phone and played a clip of himself on "the news." He held it up proudly, volume cranked just loud enough for everyone at the table to hear his own voice coming through the speakers: "WLFI is freedom. WLFI is rails. WLFI is the future of finance." He froze the video and looked around. "Do I look like I know what I'm talking about?" The table erupted—booming laughter, champagne flutes sloshing over white linen.

"Doesn't matter if you know," Don Jr. wheezed, wiping his eyes. "What matters is they think you do. And they do. Perception, baby. Perception is reality." The smugness was thick enough to choke on. One of the VCs—sharp suit, gold watch, pupils wide from whatever was fueling him through the night—leaned in reverently. "Gentlemen, congratulations. You're not just in the news. You are the news."

Around them, aides were already working the angles. A young staffer refreshed Twitter feeds, rattling off trending hashtags: #WLFI, #TrumpMoney, #OwnTheRails. Another prepped screenshots of social clips with Eric's soundbite, cut against flashy graphics and EDM beats, destined for viral churn. Witkoff kept up his nervous tick scribbling on the back of napkins, sliding it across the table to one of the hedge funders. Even in triumph, he treated everything like a deal memo.

They toasted again, glasses clinking with that particular satisfaction of men who believed they had outsmarted the entire system. The chandeliers glowed above them, gold light reflecting off their smirks. And in that room, for those men, it wasn't about truth. It wasn't about legality. It wasn't even about money. It was about the high of being untouchable.

As the laughter died down, Witkoff leaned forward, voice low but laced with pride. "You know the beauty of it?" he said, tapping the folded Journal with one finger. "Half the stories out there aren't even written by journalists. They're ours. Press releases laundered through PR firms, reprinted word-for-word. The bylines don't matter. Nobody checks."

Eric smirked, still scrolling through clips of himself. "They don't need to check. Once it's on the ticker, it's real. You can't fight that." Don Jr. raised his glass again, a smirk curling at his lips. "Welcome to the new central bank, gentlemen. We don't just print money. We print headlines." The table erupted, arrogance hanging in the air like smoke.

What stuck with me weren't the jokes. Not the champagne. Not the bragging about TV spots. It was the quiet confession, buried under laughter: They weren't winning because of the truth. They were winning because they'd hacked the story.

Chapter 19: Manufactured Headlines

I had to know how deep it went. The allusion at Mar-a-Lago kept echoing in my head: We don't just print money. We print headlines. It sounded like a joke. But it wasn't. So I started tracing. First stop: the press releases. WLFI's "media room" looked legit— sleek logos, downloadable PDFs, boilerplate about freedom and rails. But when I cross-checked, the same paragraphs turned up in Bloomberg "analysis," MarketWatch "reports," even in a CNBC chyron. They hadn't even bothered to rewrite it. PR laundering. I'd seen it before. A company pays a PR firm to ghostwrite glowing copy, then pushes it to wire services where it gets scraped by newsrooms desperate for filler. The story looks like reporting, but it's just advertising with better fonts. WLFI had mastered the trick.

Then came the ad buys. Exchanges weren't just slapping WLFI logos around for fun—they were paid. Banner packages. Sponsored "thought leadership" interviews. I found a media kit from one outlet that offered bundles: for fifty grand you could buy "coverage placement" in their crypto vertical, complete with a guaranteed headline. WLFI was buying bundles by the dozen.

And it didn't stop there. Podcasts. YouTubers. Even legacy outlets like Forbes, where "contributors" published puff pieces that read like fan fiction. Some called WLFI "the people's coin." Others floated lines like "Trump's crypto could save the dollar." Trace them back far enough and they led to the same PR agency in New York.

The illusion was airtight. Retail investors scrolling Twitter didn't know the difference between sponsored content and journalism. Hell, half the journalists didn't either. I wrote in my notebook:

Money prints USD1.
USD1 prints WLFI.
WLFI prints headlines.
Headlines print belief.

It was a closed circuit, not of finance but of perception—a feedback loop that didn't just generate money, but manufactured legitimacy. And here's the worst part: if you followed the loop long enough, truth itself vanished. Because what happens when a news chyron gets repeated on Twitter, then quoted in Bloomberg, then referenced in a speech on the House floor? At some point, the origin doesn't matter. The repetition becomes the reality.

I sat back from the desk, palms sweaty. If WLFI could buy headlines, and headlines bought belief, then there was no such thing as objective fact anymore. Trump had always understood this better than anyone. He didn't have to build skyscrapers. He just had to stamp TRUMP on them. The building became real in people's minds because the brand said it was real. WLFI was the same trick—except the product wasn't a tower or a steak or a university. It was money itself.

And if money is just belief... then whoever controls the story controls the value. WLFI hadn't hacked finance. They hadn't hacked politics. They had hacked reality.

Chapter 20: Receipts

I didn't want speculation anymore. I wanted something undeniable—proof that WLFI wasn't just lucky with headlines, but manufacturing them. That's how I found Claire. She wasn't a whistleblower type—no trench coat, no hushed paranoia. She was just tired. A mid-tier financial reporter, bylines scattered across Bloomberg, Forbes, and MarketWatch. The kind of person who knew how the sausage was made. We met in a booth at a K Street diner, the kind of place where lobbyists and interns drank the same burnt coffee.

"You think WLFI hacked the press?" she said, no preamble, no small talk. "They didn't hack it. They used it the way it was built." She slid a manila folder across the table. Inside were printouts: press releases, email threads from PR firms, draft copy with tracked changes. Highlighted in yellow were paragraphs that matched, word for word, with stories that had run under her byline. "That Bloomberg 'analysis' everyone keeps quoting?" she said. "Straight from a WLFI media kit. I barely touched it. Changed two verbs, swapped a headline. It was live in an hour."

She flipped to another page. A Forbes contributor piece that had gone viral. "Ghostwritten by WLFI's PR team. The 'author' just slapped his name on it." I turned the pages slowly, feeling the weight build. This wasn't conspiracy-theory nonsense. It was receipts.

Claire stirred her coffee but didn't drink it. Her eyes looked flat, resigned. "This isn't corruption. It's indifference. Editors don't care if it's true. They care if it's fast and if it clicks. WLFI knows that. They flood the zone with copy, and the industry's too thin, too tired, too hungry to resist." She leaned in, her tone sharper now. "And here's the kicker: it doesn't matter if it's positive or negative. Every headline feeds them. A FOX hit, a Bloomberg puff piece, even a skeptical op-ed—it all keeps the name alive. And in their world? The name is the value."

The folder sat heavy in my hands, undeniable proof of what I'd been circling for weeks: WLFI didn't just control the token. They controlled the narrative. They didn't build skyscrapers. They just stamped their name on them. And now, they were stamping reality itself.

Chapter 21: The Listings Game

The morning it went live, my feed was wall-to-wall WLFI:
"WLFI is live! WLFI is real! This is history!" I sat at my kitchen
table, half-drained mug of coffee in front of me, staring at the
chyron looping on TV: "WLFI Achieves Major Exchange
Listings." To the average viewer, it looked like validation. If
Binance listed it, if Gate listed it, if Bitget put it front and center—
WLFI must be legitimate. That's the trick. That's the illusion. But
I'd been around crypto long enough to know: listings aren't
endorsements. They're transactions. I called an old contact in
compliance at a mid-tier exchange. We hadn't spoken in years, but
when I dropped WLFI's name, there was a pause—long enough to
let me know I'd hit a nerve.

"They're just another token," he said carefully. "But tokens
like WLFI don't get listed. They buy their way in."

"How much?" I asked.

He chuckled bitterly. "Depends on the exchange. Mid-tier
can be a few hundred grand. Binance? Seven figures. Plus, volume
guarantees. Plus, market makers to juice the books. Nothing goes
live without that."

Business Insider once reported that ICO projects paid
anywhere from $50,000 to $1 million for listings—and that was
years ago. Industry chatter since has only pushed those numbers
higher. On Binance, seven figures isn't rumor; it's the cost of
entry. On paper, it looked like a dream come true. Binance. Gate.
Bitget. WLFI banners shining like neon signs at the edge of the
digital strip. Every homepage screamed the same thing: legitimacy.
And people believed it.

I watched retail pile in, live, on Etherscan and
DexScreener. Wallets buying in bursts—$200, $500, $2,000 at a
time. Ordinary people with ordinary money, chasing the same
promise we'd all heard before: don't miss it like you missed
Bitcoin. The bots let them think they were winning. Orders filled
instantly, price ticking up, wallets swelling with WLFI.
Screenshots hit Twitter: "In at thirty cents—this is going to the
moon!" For a moment, it looked real.

But then came the flips. Bots sniped ahead, skimming profit in microseconds. Wash trades pumped volume without value. The very same exchanges that listed WLFI juiced the numbers, creating the illusion of momentum while the insiders quietly unloaded into the froth. I traced one wallet—a buy of nearly $2,000 worth of WLFI, neatly packaged into smaller trades. Within an hour, the value had halved. The tokens were dumped into an offshore wallet, leaving the buyer holding a bag worth less than rent.

And yet the headlines didn't stop. CNBC still flashed "Record WLFI Volume." X still trended #WLFItoTheMoon. Retail still bought in, convinced the dip was a chance to double down. It reminded me of being a kid at a carnival. The barkers yelling, the lights flashing, the smell of popcorn thick in the air. You throw your money at the ring toss, knowing deep down the bottles are spaced just far enough apart that the rings can never land. But the illusion is so good, the lights so bright, that you believe you'll be the one who wins.

WLFI was the carnival—except this time, the prizes weren't stuffed animals. They were people's savings.

I sat back, notebook open, watching the numbers flicker. The cycle was merciless.

Retail buys the dream.
Bots scalp the spread.
Exchanges bank the fees.
Insiders cash the exit.

The house always won. And the only thing retail walked away with was the illusion they'd been in the game at all.

Chapter 22: Listed

The boys treated it like a coronation. Gone was the Mar-a-Lago opulence. Now, it was a glass-walled penthouse in Miami, the skyline glittering below like a trove of gemstones. Screens mounted on the walls replayed the same loop: "WLFI Now Listed on Major Exchanges." Binance. Gate. Bitget. Even a whispered tease about Coinbase "in talks."

Eric strutted through the room like he'd just been handed the keys to Fort Knox. He planted himself in front of one screen, hands on his hips, basking in the glow of the WLFI logo next to the Binance banner. "Do you see this?" he said, voice cracking with excitement. "It's like we just went public. But better. No IPO. No bankers. Just us."

Don Jr. slapped him on the back, laughing. "Binance is basically the NYSE of crypto. You can't not take us seriously now. I mean—this is it. Legitimacy." A bottle of champagne popped in the corner. Glasses rose, filled, clinked.

Witkoff, direct as ever, cut through the noise: "Listings aren't charity. They're partnerships. Exchanges don't just let anyone in. They know WLFI drives volume—and volume drives fees. This is mutual." Eric beamed; glass lifted high. "To the exchanges. To the rails. To WLFI on every damn screen in the world!" The toast echoed across the penthouse. To them, this was the moment WLFI crossed the Rubicon. No more outsider story. They were in. And for everyone reading headlines the next day, it looked exactly like that: inevitability.

Chapter 23: The Money Machine

I kept circling back to the same question: if this was decentralized, then who was really in control? The headlines offered one answer: "Alt5 Sigma Raises $1.5 Billion to Establish WLFI Treasury Strategy." Deep in the fine print lay the real twist—half the proceeds were WLFI tokens, the other half cash. A $1.5 billion closed loop masquerading as capital. This wasn't traditional investing. It was transference of power. ALT5 wasn't just a holder—they became the treasury. The banker. The gatekeeper.

And then came the kicker: Zach Witkoff, co-founder and CEO of WLFI, was named Chairman of ALT5's board. Eric Trump was appointed director, with other WLFI-linked figures taking senior roles—all central architects now stewards of the system. World Liberty Financial—the same entity that created WLFI—acted as the lead investor.

I stared at the filings, on-chain data, and media releases. Alt5 didn't control WLFI in spite of the Trump family. They controlled it because of the Trump family. It was dizzying. Imagine the Fed—but with the President's sons on the board, every dollar printed flowing back into their own pockets. And this time, it wasn't metaphor—it was happening, in public, with ticker symbols and prospectuses to prove it. I wrote in my notebook:

WLFI mints USD1, skimming profit.
USD1 flows into the treasury, wrapped in Alt5's reserves.
Alt5 holds this WLFI as collateral, selling or releasing when it suits them.
The illusion of independence vanishes when you see the names.

Every token someone bought on Binance or Gate, every flash headline about record volume, every TikTok chanting #WLFItoTheMoon—it all circled back to Alt5. To a single entity controlling more than 7% of the total supply. The slogan had always been: You are in control. The polished promise of DeFi. But staring at these documents, I wrote the only phrase that could still ring true: You are not in control.

Retail never was. Exchanges weren't. Not even Washington, with its carefully named GENIUS and CLARITY bills. So then, who was? That question ate at me: Alt5 wasn't a distant investor—it was staffed and steered by WLFI's own creators. They hadn't just programmed a system; they built it, branded it, then pulled the levers. I shut my laptop, the screen's glow still seared in my vision. The money machine was running, gears greased with branding and belief. And it wasn't running for me.

Chapter 24: The Human Cost

For weeks, I'd been scribbling at fever pitch: unlock cycles, bot wars, Alt5's treasury grip—it all formed a system of smoke and mirrors designed to enrich the few and fleece the many. But until now, it had been numbers on a page. Theory. A thesis. Then I saw it play out in real time. Screens filled with "WLFI surges past 30–46 cents!" CNBC ran the chyron: "Trump-Backed Token Smashes Records." Retail traders flooded in—*Don't miss it like you missed Bitcoin!*—only to face a brutal reversal. WLFI plunged 30–50% within hours.

I dove into forums, Telegram threads, comment sections—finding heartbreak, not hype. "I just put in $1,200," wrote one user. "Thought it would grow… now it's half that." A former veteran shared an IRA snapshot: "$15k into WLFI. Trump wouldn't back a scam," he typed. His tone cracked days later: "I sold. Lost most of it. I can't keep doing this." A young mom on TikTok grinned confidently: "Second chance—missed Bitcoin, but not this time." She filmed flashing a $5,000 purchase. Comments flooded—queen energy! HODL!—until her account fell silent.

Then there was Andrew Tate—real, public, documented. He got liquidated for $67,500 on WLFI futures… then doubled down within minutes. Profits or losses, either way, it was free marketing.

All of this was real. People I could've met. Names erased for privacy, but not their losses. And while they bled, the Wall Street Journal estimated the Trump family's WLFI paper gain at $5 billion that day. That number lodged like glass in my throat. A flawless design.

I let the sorrow wash over me. Dejected, I wrote:

Retail is the product.
Their money is the liquidity.
Their losses are the fuel.

The slogans—*You Are in Control, Own the Rails*—looked gaudy now, like graffiti on a crime scene. And for the first time, what replaced paranoia was rage—sharp, burning, justified. This wasn't an accident. It was the outcome they engineered: the system was feeding, and its prey was earnest people. I closed the notebook, bile rising. The machine was running. And real people were being chewed alive.

Chapter 25: Losers Fuel Liquidity

It wasn't in a press release. It wasn't shouted on CNN. It came from the shadows—private dinners, Telegram leaks, off-the-record whispers among men who think the microphones are off. I cobbled it together from attendees—hedge funders, mid-tier exchange execs, the sycophants orbiting the Trumps like moths around chandeliers. Different vantage points, but the same tone. The smirk. The contempt. These weren't talks about governance or revolution. They were about losers.

One attendee said plainly: *"The vibe was that retail was the engine. They needed them to lose. That's where the liquidity comes from."* Another described Witkoff pacing in front of a screen, diagramming treasury flows, circling the word volume like it was sacred writ. *"Doesn't matter if the price moves up or down,"* he recalled. *"What matters is the churn. Losers keep the churn alive."*

Then came the line you can't unhear—from a man raised in public spectacle but speaking in private, smug and casual: *"They actually toasted to it—glasses raised, talking about how every sell-off, every wrecked account, every panic dump—that was the grease in the gears. Losers keep the machine alive."* Not for cameras, not for press. Just said like bankers laughing over cigars.

Then Don Jr., lean and relaxed, drink in hand: "Doesn't matter what happens—they always come back. New losers replace the old ones. That's the beauty of it." The table roared.

I sat back later, notebook filled with fragments and arrows, none of it public—but the tone darker than you'd expect. They didn't see retail as peers. They saw retail as coal.

If it took burning a teacher's savings, a veteran's retirement, or a mom's credit card debt to keep the engine running—that was just liquidity. They laughed about it. And that laugh stayed with me long after the sources fell silent.*

---

* In real-world corridors of crypto, sentiment like "retail = exit liquidity" is not invention. On X, crypto investigator ZachXBT recently lambasted XRP holders as just that—"exit liquidity" for insiders—highlighting the transactional contempt that sometimes underpins token launches.

Chapter 26: The Scale of It

I closed my laptop and just sat there, staring at the dark reflection of my own face in the screen. The laughter still echoed—not the words alone, but the tone. That smug, casual contempt. The way they talked about wrecked savings accounts like poker chips, as if people's lives were just numbers on a ledger. "Losers keep the machine alive." That was it. The whole model distilled into one sentence.

I thought of the teacher in Ohio, the veteran in Florida, the mom in Texas. Real people who believed the slogans—You are in control. Own the rails. They weren't in control. They were fuel. And if that was the playbook here—what happened when WLFI scaled it? I flipped open my notebook, pages scrawled with months of scribbles:

Bots faking volume.
Exchanges juicing numbers.
Alt5 holding billions in supply.
Press releases recycled as headlines.
Retail wreckage feeding liquidity.

All of it—every gear and cog—ran on the same principle: *you are not in control.*
And it didn't stop at borders.

USD1 was already spreading—pairs on Binance, mentions in Africa, integrations across smaller exchanges where regulations were weak and hope was high. These were the markets where people clung hardest to the promise of stability. A token stamped with Trump's name could look like safety.

It hit me like a gut punch: this wasn't just retail wreckage in Ohio or Texas. This was systemic. Entire economies could be roped into the same illusion. Losers wouldn't just be individuals anymore—they'd be nations. And the Trumps knew it. That's why they laughed. Because they weren't celebrating a payday. They were celebrating inevitability.

This is not a market. This is extraction. And it's going global.

This wasn't just about crypto anymore. This was about power. And the people who had it were laughing at the rest of us.

The room was quiet now. Just me at my desk, lamp casting long shadows across scattered notes. The noise of the day—screens flashing, headlines blaring, villains laughing—had finally gone still. And in that silence, the shape of it became clear. WLFI wasn't a coin. It wasn't even a company. It was a bank.

The filings and press releases made it plain: Alt5's $1.5 billion treasury deal, with Eric Trump and Zach Witkoff on the board. More than half the token supply tied up under their control. Governance votes steered by insiders who already owned the rails. USD1 minted with every transaction, fees siphoned upward. This wasn't decentralization. It was consolidation. A system dressed up as freedom but bent toward one axis of power.

I remember opening my first bank account at the Children's Bank of America. What genius came up with that name? My dad walked me through the big stone building, the one with marble counters and brass pens chained to the desk. He handed me my birthday money and let me slide it across to the teller. The place smelled of polish and permanence. There were rules, guardrails. A sense that money was protected by something larger than any one person.

WLFI mirrored that same architecture—but hollowed out. No stone walls, no permanence, no guardrails. Just branding. Just a handful of men in boardrooms and ballrooms, toasting each other while ordinary people lost their shirts.

It was the central bank of crypto. A private one.

I carved the words into my notebook, pressing the ink so hard it cut into the page:

The illusion of freedom.
The reality of control.
The first private central bank.

And as the ink dried, the weight of it settled. This wasn't about traders hoping to flip a profit, or exchanges skimming fees. This was about power—consolidated, branded, scaled. A system that looked like freedom on the surface but funneled everything back to the same handful of men at the top.

The realization wasn't dramatic. It wasn't paranoia. It was worse: it was clarity.
This wasn't just about traders or exchanges. This was about power. And it was scaling.

Steve closes his notebook.
The pen torn the page where he scrawled the last line:

The illusion of freedom. The reality of control. The first private central bank.

He exhales, hand trembling—not from exhaustion, but recognition. And then the voice shifts…

Chapter 27: You Are Steve

You've been reading this like it's a thriller. Some mix of scandal and politics that couldn't possibly touch you. That's the lie. The comfort. But look again.

The headlines I laid out—you've seen them. CNBC: "WLFI Achieves Major Exchange Listings." Wall Street Journal: "Trump Family's Paper Gain Hits $5 Billion." TikTok clips of influencers chanting #WLFItoTheMoon. You scrolled past them. Maybe you felt that flicker of curiosity. Should I get in?

The numbers—100% real. WLFI surged past 31¢ at launch, then collapsed to 21¢ within hours. Andrew Tate really lost $67,500 on WLFI futures before bragging he'd doubled down.

The structures—you can verify them yourself. Alt5's $1.5 billion treasury. Eric Trump on the board. Zach Witkoff as chairman. More than half the WLFI supply locked in one place. Every transaction minting USD1, fees siphoned upward.

These aren't just notes. They're facts.

And that means something uncomfortable: **You are Steve**.

The Grift in Plain Sight

WLFI's brilliance isn't secrecy—it's spectacle. The machine works because you believe what you see: volume, headlines, logos, influencers.
You were told: You are in control.
But every fact says otherwise:
- Bots control the trades.
- Exchanges control the volume.
- Alt5 controls the supply.
- The Trumps control the bank.

And all the while, retail investors—teachers, veterans, parents—lose their savings to a system designed to need losers.

Losers don't break the machine. Losers keep it alive.

The Mirror

And here's the gut punch: **<u>none of it is illegal</u>**.
Alt5's treasury is disclosed. Listings were paid for. PR was laundered through official wires. Headlines were technically accurate.

The machine isn't hiding—it's humming in broad daylight.

Which means this doesn't end tomorrow. Or next week. Or after one crash, or ten. As long as people believe, the machine runs. And belief is the one thing WLFI has mastered.

So, this is the mirror: you are not reading about Steve. You are reading about yourself.

You are the one scrolling headlines, watching prices whip, muttering are you kidding me? as villains toast to "losers fueling liquidity."

You are Steve. And just like him, you are not in control.

No catharsis. No twist. Just the truth: this isn't history. It isn't prediction.

It's the present tense.

The machine is here. And you're inside it.

Epilogue 1: One Week in the Wild

(September 9, 2025)

At the time of this writing, seven days have passed since World Liberty Financial entered the market. That short span is enough to reveal the early architecture of what it is becoming.

The launch began with a promise of scarcity: a cap of 16 billion tokens. It was a number that suggested discipline, the kind of limit investors could trust. Within days, that number was discarded. The supply expanded to 100 billion tokens, executed in code but consequential in value. The effect was immediate: Donald J. Trump's personal allocation, once modest by comparison, now represented over $5 billion in paper wealth.

Market reaction followed a familiar curve. On opening day, WLFI climbed to $0.32, implying a total valuation of $32 billion. That figure placed it, briefly, in the same conversation as major financial institutions. But the spike was short-lived. By the end of the week the price stabilized in the $0.20–$0.24 range. Billions in retail wealth still evaporated for those who chased the peak, while insiders who had entered at fractions of a penny retained extraordinary gains. In some cases, a $10,000 early position remained worth several million.

Around these market movements, the personalities surfaced. Justin Sun appeared, offering support while hinting at blacklists — a reminder that familiar names in crypto often reemerge whenever capital pools form.

The essential lesson of the week is structural, not theatrical. WLFI behaved less like a digital asset and more like an institution. Its mechanics echoed central banking:

- Expand supply when necessary.

- Control liquidity through the treasury.

- Establish a floor by decision rather than discovery.

Retail traders may have seen a volatile coin. Insiders saw a framework: a privately controlled monetary authority, functioning in ways the Federal Reserve might recognize.

In one week, WLFI demonstrated what it intends to be. Not a speculative meme, but a prototype — the contours of a private central bank taking form on-chain.

Epilogue 2: USD1 Cracks the Surface

If WLFI was the visible launch, USD1 was the quiet foundation beneath it. It entered the market as a stablecoin — a digital dollar designed to mirror the U.S. dollar at a one-to-one ratio. By definition, such an asset is not supposed to move. One dollar must always equal one dollar.

This week, that expectation broke. USD1 slipped. The decline was small, measured in cents, but symbolically it was large. A stablecoin is not judged by how far it falls, but by the fact that it falls at all. The slip revealed two things: that the peg is not absolute, and that WLFI has built a system designed to profit when it is tested.

The economics are straightforward. Every time a USD1 token is issued or redeemed, WLFI captures a margin. That margin expands when the peg wavers. At $250 million in circulation, even a 0.5% spread across issuance, redemption, and churn equates to over $1 million a week in revenue. If circulation scales to $1 billion, the same math produces roughly $50 million annually — income generated independently of WLFI's token price.

In effect, every USD1 is not only a dollar; it is a loan to WLFI. Holders may view it as digital cash, but the issuer views it as float, available for profit.

The significance of this became clearer as outside observers began to change their framing. A Blockworks report described WLFI as the "central bank of crypto." That description matters. It signals a shift in perception from hype to institution. What had been promoted as innovation now carried the vocabulary of governance and monetary authority.

The concern is not the volatility itself. It is the normalization of a private organization controlling a currency peg and capturing profit from its movement. The lesson of the week is simple: a dollar is no longer a dollar when its value depends on private discretion.

Epilogue 3: And on the Eighth Day

If the first week revealed the mechanics, the eighth day revealed the politics.

Eric Trump lost his board seat. The move was sudden, symbolic, and instructive. In traditional governance, board reshuffling is routine. In this case, it underscored that WLFI is not a public institution but a family enterprise, where power is both inherited and contested.

The metaphor is irresistible: And on the eighth day, God said—Eric, you are no longer needed.

The loss mattered less for what Eric did than for what it represented. WLFI's board was always more about optics than function. The decisions — token expansion, liquidity control, governance votes — were never diffuse. They traced back to the same concentrated center. Eric's removal clarified that even inside the dynasty, not all voices carry equal weight.

Meanwhile, the messaging from the remaining figures remained consistent.

- Zach Witkoff framed it as empire-building, declaring that Trump was "building an empire again," this time in money rather than real estate.

- Donald Trump Jr. spoke in terms of rebellion, calling WLFI "bigger than the Fed," a declaration that blurred the line between political theater and monetary ambition.

- Eric Trump, before his exit, offered the most patriotic gloss, describing WLFI as "America First finance" — a phrase that sounded populist but functioned as branding for a private mint.

Together, these statements reveal intent rather than accident. WLFI was never simply an experiment in cryptocurrency. It was constructed to operate as a central bank in private hands, with family and close allies positioned as its governors.

The lesson of the eighth day is that the institution is dynastic, not democratic. Its design mirrors a state, but its governance reflects a household.

Epilogue 4: The Central Bank of Crypto

By the close of the first week, the outlines were clear. WLFI was not behaving like a typical digital asset. It was assuming the functions of a monetary authority.

The mechanics were consistent: expand supply at will, manage liquidity through a central treasury, and stabilize value by decree rather than discovery. USD1, operating in the background, provided the rails — a stablecoin that generated revenue with each issuance and redemption. WLFI and USD1 together formed a closed circuit: the coin feeding the bank, the bank controlling the coin.

The flow of profit was upward. Retail investors absorbed the volatility; insiders collected the margin. Each wobble of USD1's peg created arbitrage. Each new partnership added a toll. Each governance decision reinforced control.

The resemblance to a central bank is not metaphorical. It is functional. A balance sheet, a float, an issuer of currency, a mechanism to influence value. But this bank is not sovereign. It is private. Its signatures are not elected officials; they are the Trump family and their closest allies.

The outside world has begun to name it. Headlines have called WLFI the first central bank of crypto. That is accurate. What began as speculation now operates as structure. What appeared to be hype now resembles governance.

At this moment, it cannot be stopped.

The first central bank of crypto exists — and it belongs to them.

For additional information: WLFireside
(https://substack.com/@wlfireside)

Bibliography

Legislation & Congressional Record

U.S. Congress. 'CLARITY Act' discussion draft and related coverage. Axios, May 22, 2024. Available via: https://www.axios.com (see crypto legislation reporting).

U.S. Congress. 'GENIUS Act' discussion draft and related coverage. Axios, May 22, 2024. Available via: https://www.axios.com (see crypto legislation reporting).

U.S. House of Representatives. H.R. 5403 — CBDC Anti-Surveillance State Act (118th Congress). House passage reported May 23, 2024. Congress.gov.

U.S. House of Representatives. H.R. 1919 — CBDC Anti-Surveillance State Act (119th Congress). Introduced March 11, 2025. Congress.gov.

Congressional Record. 'CBDC Anti-Surveillance State Act' debate and floor proceedings — July 17, 2025. GPO/CR, CREC-2025-07-17.

Broadcast & Interviews (Public Statements)

Fox Business (Video). 'Ohio congressman sees cryptocurrency as "freedom money".' Interview with Rep. Warren Davidson, October 21, 2021.

Donald Trump Jr., at the Ondo Summit in New York City, February 6, 2025 CoinDesk

Fox News (Video). 'Rep. Warren Davidson: The Fed should be nowhere near your wallet.' Segment, July 2023.

Bloomberg Television. 'Balance of Power' — Interview clip with Rep. Warren Davidson on crypto and 'freedom money', November 24, 2021.

TheStreet (Interview/Article). 'Rep. Warren Davidson on Bitcoin: It's freedom money; don't "Dogecoin" the dollar.' November 24, 2021.

AOL. "Trump Family's World Liberty Financial Venture Could Reshape Banking, Says Steve Witkoff." *AOL News*, September 2025.

Donald Trump Jr. "World Liberty Financial is not some meme coin, it's the governance backbone of a real ecosystem changing how money moves." *X (formerly Twitter)*, September 2025.

AOL. "Don Jr. Says Family Got into Crypto Because They Saw the Future of Banking in World Liberty Financial." *Yahoo Finance/AOL News*, September 2025.

Blockworks. "World Liberty Financial is Perfecting TradFi." September 2025.

DLNews. "Trump Media's $6B Crypto.com Partnering." August 2025.

Trump Jr., Donald. Public remarks and media coverage of Trump family crypto involvement, 2024–2025.

Trump, Eric. Public remarks and media coverage of Trump family crypto involvement, 2024–2025.

Witkoff, Steven. Commentary and reporting on WLFI governance, Alt5 acquisition, and financial infrastructure framing, 2024–2025.

Technical & Academic Sources

Nakamoto, S. (2008). 'Bitcoin: A Peer-to-Peer Electronic Cash System.' https://bitcoin.org/bitcoin.pdf

Buterin, V. (2013). 'Ethereum Whitepaper: A Next-Generation Smart Contract & Decentralized Application Platform.' https://ethereum.org/en/whitepaper/

Daian, P., et al. (2019). 'Flash Boys 2.0: Frontrunning, Transaction Reordering, and Consensus Instability in Decentralized Exchanges.' https://arxiv.org/abs/1904.05234

Cong, L. W., Li, X., Tang, K., & Yang, Y. (2022). 'Detecting and Quantifying Crypto Wash Trading.' Tokenomics 2021 (OASIcs). https://doi.org/10.4230/OASIcs.Tokenomics.2021.10

MEV & Orderflow (Industry Documentation)

Flashbots Docs. 'Overview; MEV-Boost Introduction; MEV-Share Introduction; Flashbots Auction Overview.' https://docs.flashbots.net/

Flashbots Writings. 'Beginner's Guide to mev-boost.' https://writings.flashbots.net/beginners-guide-mevboost

Stablecoins & CBDCs (Policy/Research)

BIS (2023). 'Stablecoins: risks, potential and regulation.' Bank for International Settlements reports.

IMF (2024). 'The Crypto Ecosystem and Financial Stability.' IMF publications on stablecoins/CBDCs.

People's Bank of China (2021). 'Progress of Research & Development of E-CNY in China' (e-CNY White Paper).

Market Data & Chain Analytics

Etherscan. 'On-chain token/contract and transaction data (Ethereum).' https://etherscan.io

DexScreener. 'Aggregated DEX pricing and liquidity.' https://dexscreener.com

Exchange Listings, Volume & Market Quality

Bitwise (2019). 'Presentation to the SEC: Analysis of Bitcoin Spot Markets (fake volume analysis).'

Forbes (2022). 'More Than Half of All Bitcoin Trades Are Fake.' Forbes Digital Assets analysis.

Business Insider (2018). 'Crypto exchanges are charging up to $1 million per ICO to list tokens.'

The Block (2019). 'Genesis Report: Blockstack's Binance arrangements (technical integration/marketing payments).'

Media Business & Sponsored Content (Context)

CNBC Brand Studio. 'Paid Content/Brand Studio Guidelines.' CNBC Advertising resources.

Forbes. 'Contributor Network & BrandVoice — advertising and contributor content guidelines.'

About the Author

Langdon Cage writes like a sociologist with a taste for trouble. Drawn by curiosity, he follows the stories most would rather leave untold—where politics blurs into finance, and spectacle covers for power. His investigative work blends narrative bite with a documentarian's edge, pulling readers inside the machinery of the age.